Magic work book

for 4 year olds

Primer Level

A-B

For the **young** beginner

Lucia Timková

ISBN-13: 978-1490997780
ISBN-10: 1490997784

Note to Teachers

Reading and writing are two of the most important ways to learn music.
To have a break after learning and playing the exercises from Magic book A and B, it is time to relax and practice the theory in 3 steps before the end of each lesson.

● Write and practice the theory that you have learned during the lesson - write the notes, letters, numbers the value of the notes.

● Play the game noughts and crosses using the symbols that you have learned to help you to remember and understand the symbols and terminology, using it in music.

● Find the note/notes on the staff/stave in different orders that you have learned and add stems to them.

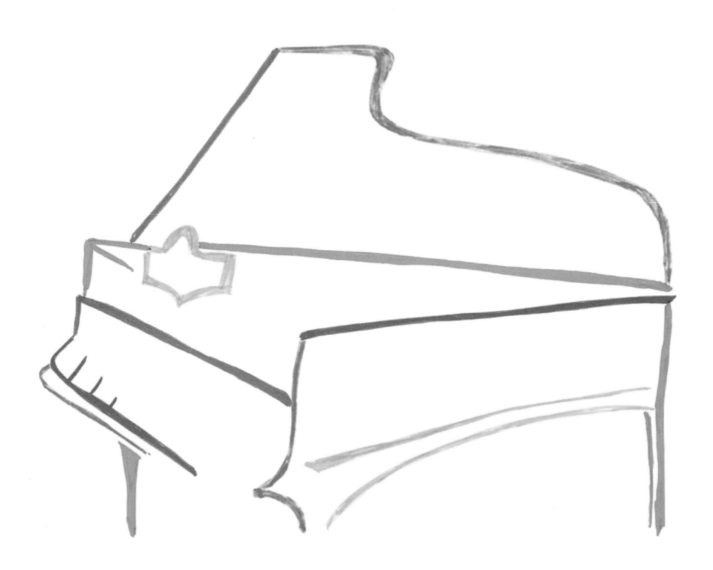

This book belongs to:

_____

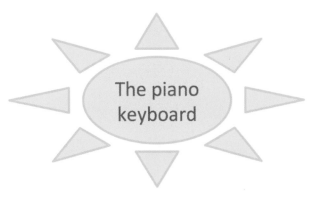

The piano keyboard

The piano keyboard has white and black keys.
The black keys are in groups of 2's and 3's.

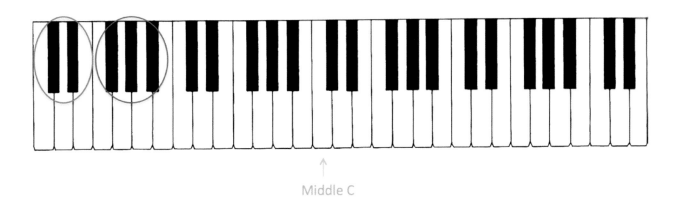

Middle C

1) Circle all the groups of two black keys with the colour red.
2) Circle all the groups of three black keys with the colour green.

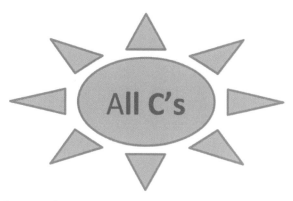

All C's

C is found to the **left** of the **TWO BLACK KEYS.**

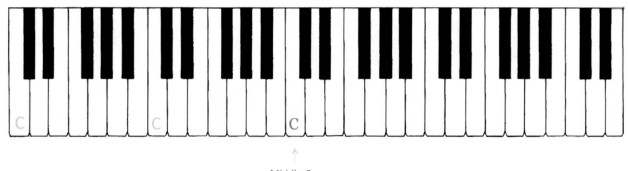

Middle C

1) **Find and draw all C notes on the keyboard.**

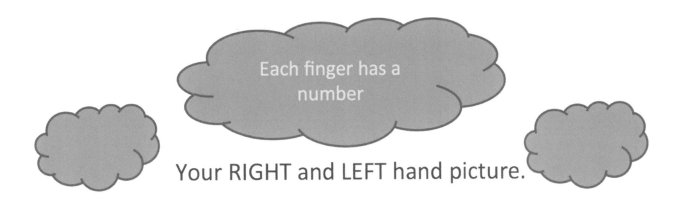

Each finger has a number

Your RIGHT and LEFT hand picture.

1) Trace your RIGHT and LEFT hand.
2) Write the number for each finger.

Stave, Staff

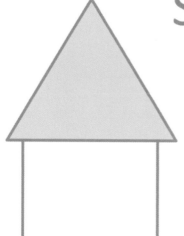

1) Draw a house –the place where people live.
2) Draw a stave/staff- the house for the notes.

Treble clef - means play with your right hand.

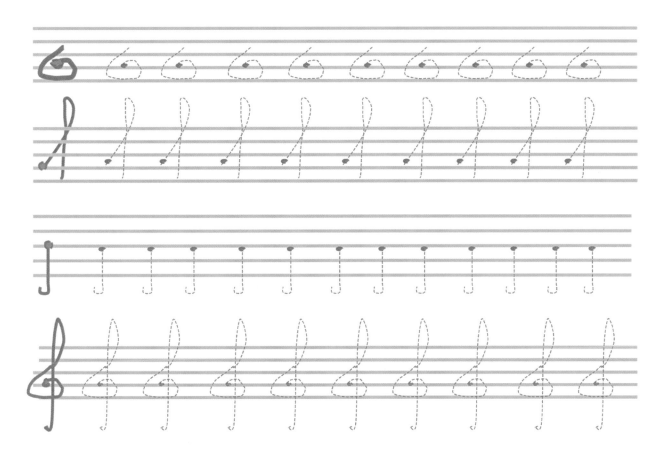

Start drawing from the blue dot.

5

Bar lines/ Bar- Measure

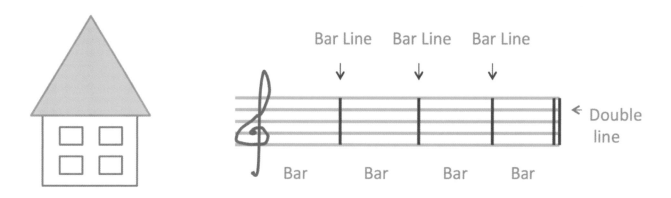

1) Draw a house with 4 rooms.
2) Draw a stave with bar lines and at the end a double line.

Time Signature

The numbers after the clef sign are called time signature.
It tells you how to count. In this book we only read the top number.

Count 4 to each bar

Count 3 to each bar

Count 2 to each bar

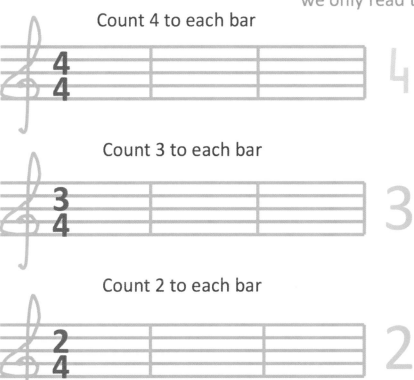

1) Draw numbers at the end of the stave.

Noughts and Crosses

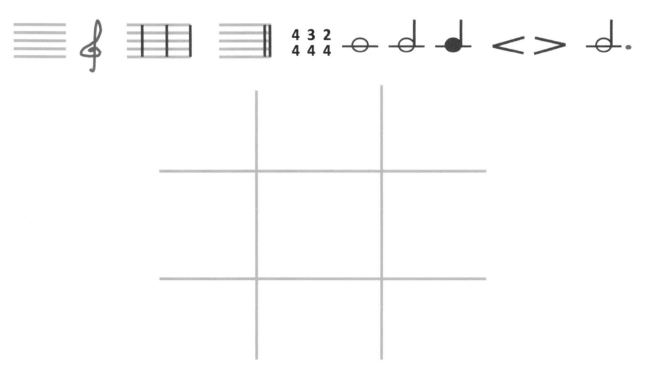

This is a game noughts and crosses and you are suppossed to play thet game always at the end of each lesson to practise and not to forget the theory.

- Write the all symbols in the empty spaces which you have already learned. (Stave, the Treble clef etc.)
- Before you circle or cross you have to say what is it and what does it mean.
- If you have three symbols which you have choosen next to each other you have a point.
- Enjoy the game with your teacher and try to win!

The rest of the free boxes are at the end of the book and than you can practise it on the board.

Finding the notes

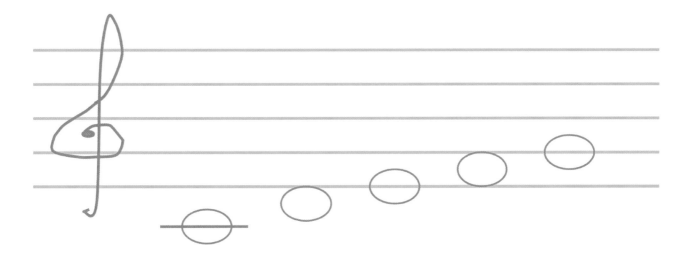

For this game you need to have 5 small circles, which should be the same size as the notes you can see above and 5 little sticks, which will be used as a stem of the note.

- Your teacher will tell you the notes that you have learned in different orders and you have to put a little circle on the correct place of the note.

- Add stems to them.

Don't forget to always play the game and practise the notes of your right hand at the end of each lesson to help you to remember the space of each note!

Whole note - Semibreve = 4 beats

$=4$

1) Draw a whole note.

Whole note C - Semibreve

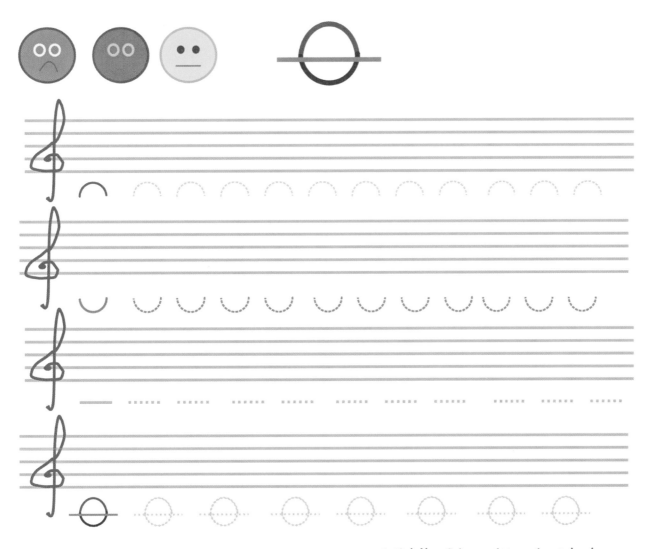

Middle C is written just below the stave on a short line. The short line is called a leger line.

C

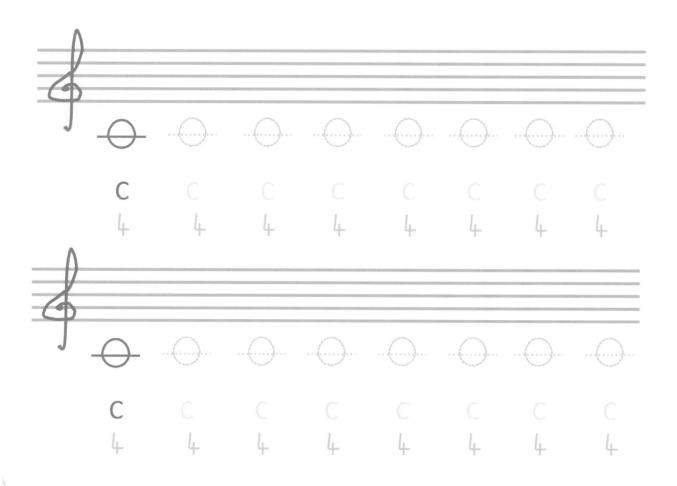

1) Draw a whole note.
2) Draw a letter.
3) Draw a number.

Half note C / Minim

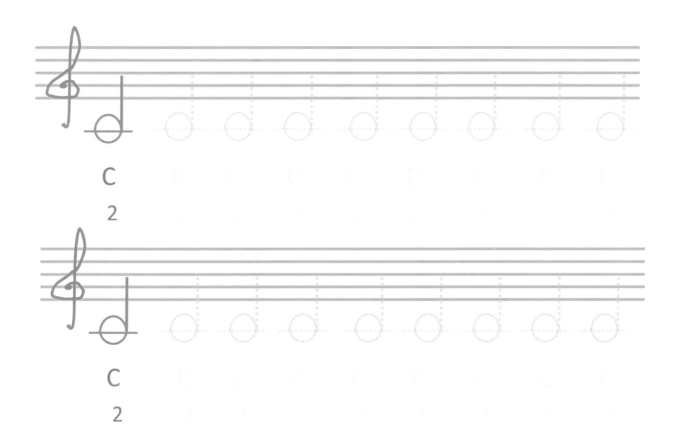

1) Draw a half note.
2) Draw a letter.
3) Draw a number.

13

Quarter note C / Crotchet

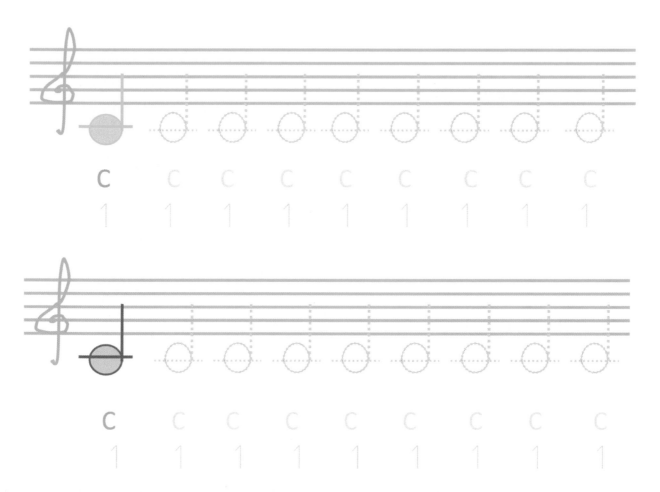

1) Draw a quarter note.
2) Draw a letter.
3) Draw a number.

C

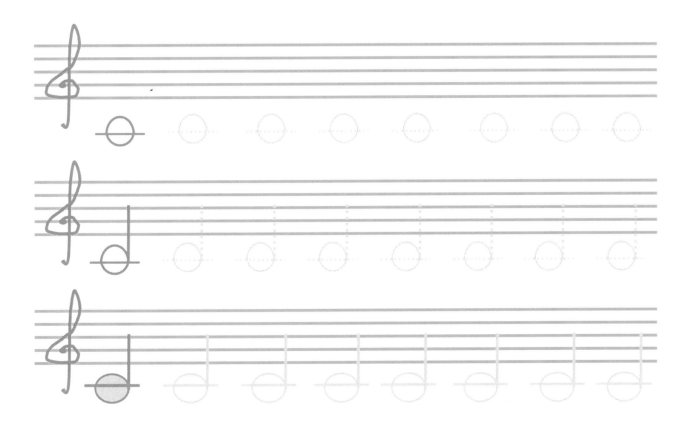

1) Draw a whole, half, quarter note.

D

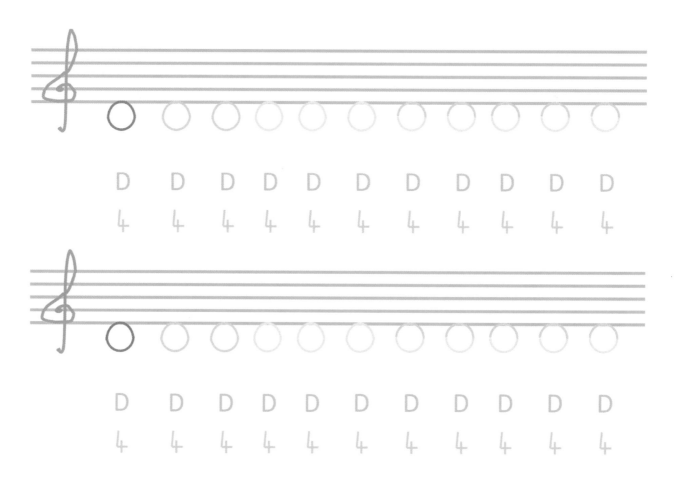

1) Draw a whole note.
2) Draw a letter.
3) Draw a number.

D

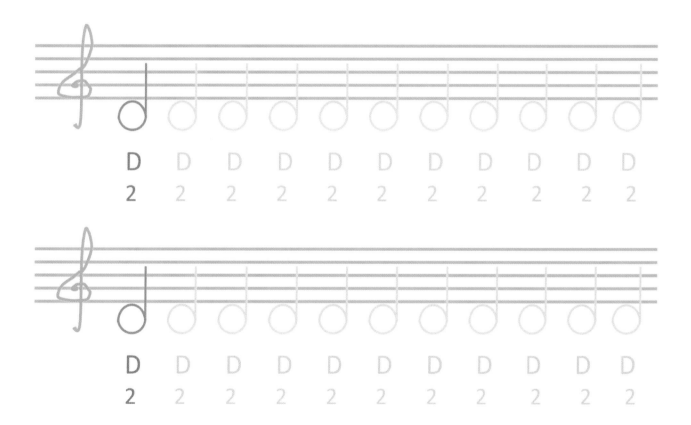

1) Draw a half note.
2) Draw a letter.
3) Draw a number.

D

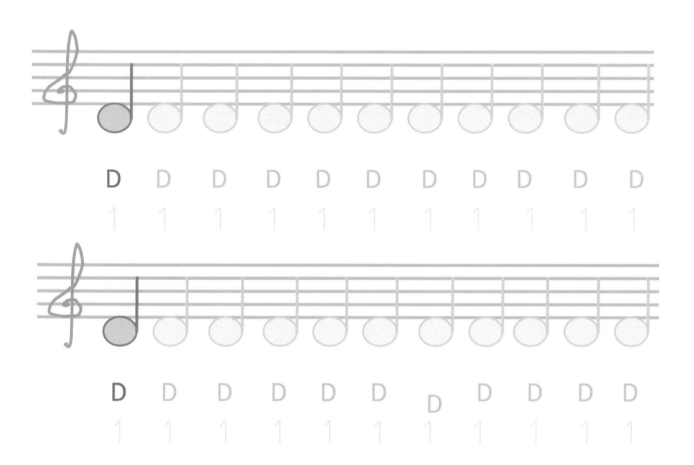

1) Draw a quarter note.
2) Draw a letter.
3) Draw a number.

D

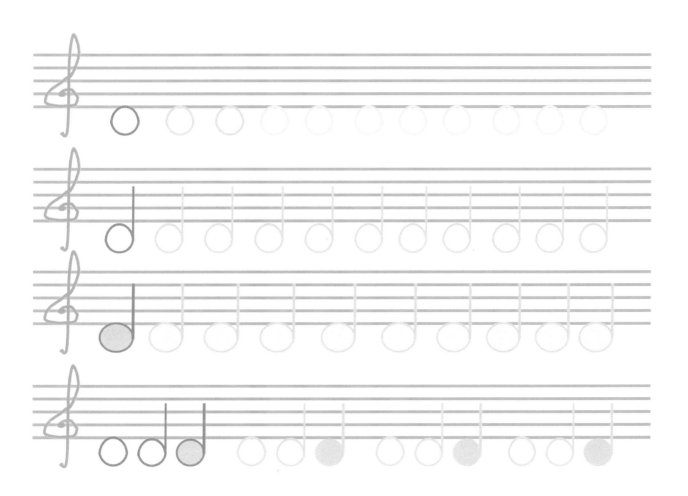

1) Draw a whole, half, quarter note.

Legato

Legato means play smootly.

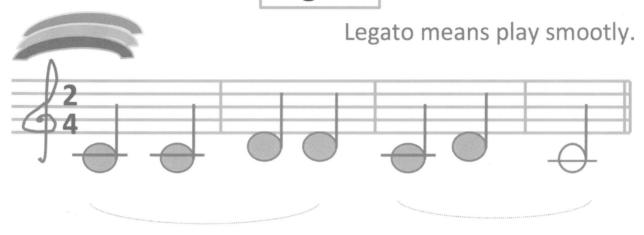

Staccato

Staccato means play shortly.

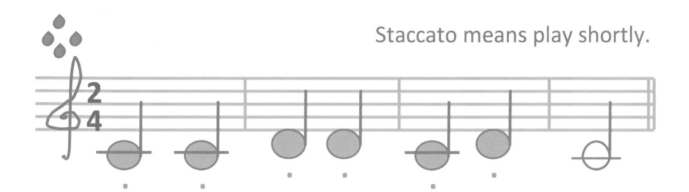

1) Draw a legato – curve.
2) Draw a staccato – dots.

E

1) Draw a whole note.
2) Draw a letter.
3) Draw a number.

21

E

E
2

E
2

1) Draw a half note.
2) Draw a letter.
3) Draw a number.

E

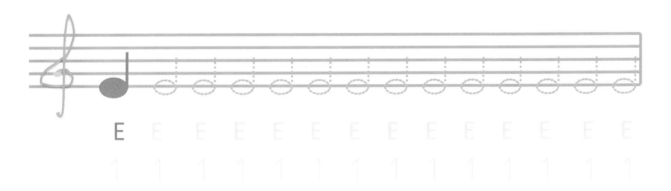

1) Draw a quarter note.
2) Draw a letter.
3) Draw a number.

E

1) Draw a whole, half, quarter note.

24

C, D, E

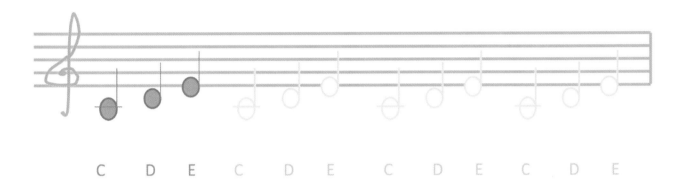

C D E C D E C D E C D E

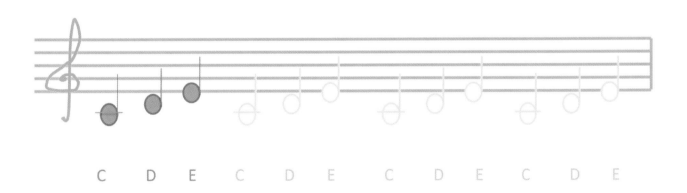

C D E C D E C D E C D E

1) Draw quarter notes.
2) Draw lettes.

25

C, D, E

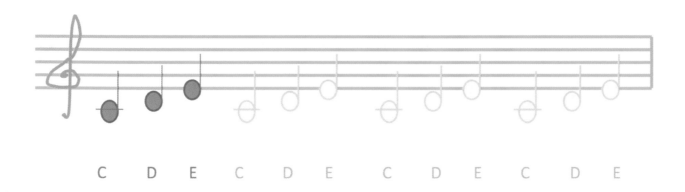

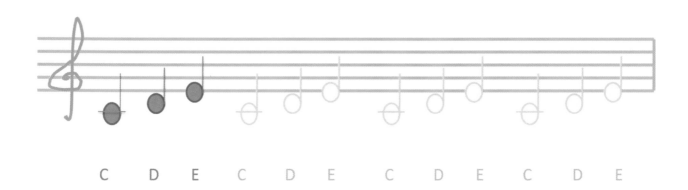

1) Draw quarter notes.
2) Draw lettes.

Crescendo Decrescendo

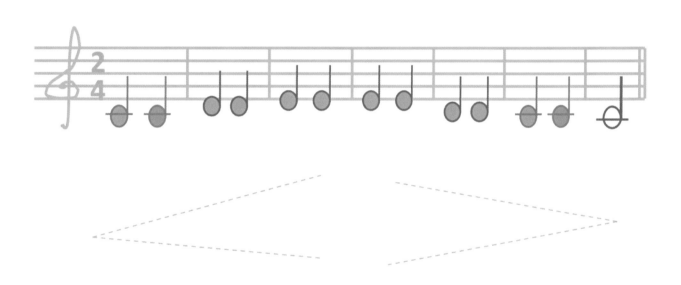

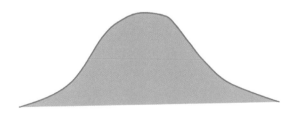

1) Draw a crescendo and decrescendo.

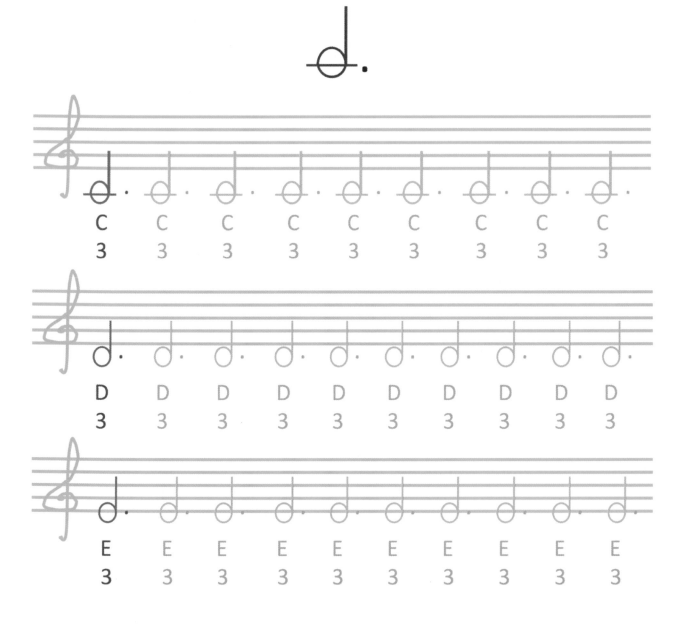

1) Draw dotted half notes / dotted

F

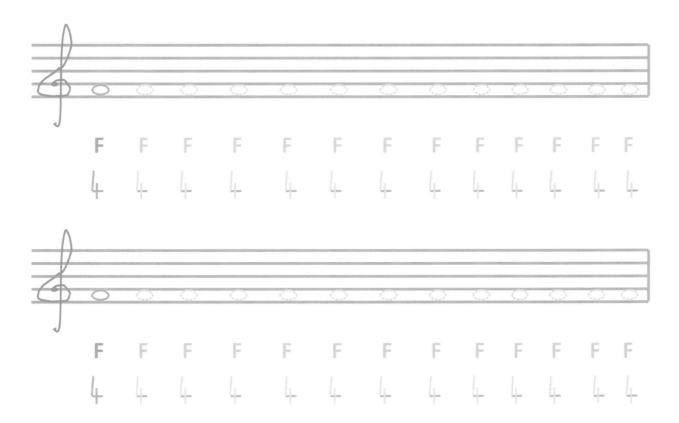

1) Draw a whole note.
2) Draw a letter.
3) Draw a number.

F

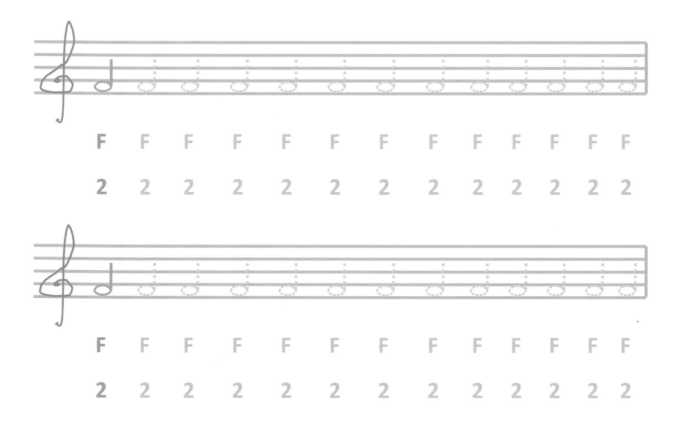

1) Draw a half note.
2) Draw a letter.
3) Draw a number.

F

1) Draw a quarter note.
2) Draw a letter.
3) Draw a number.

G

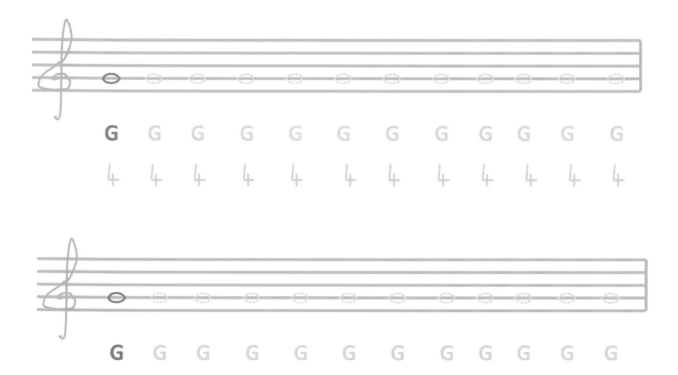

1) Draw a whole note.
2) Draw a letter.
3) Draw a number.

G

1) Draw a half note.
2) Draw a letter.
3) Draw a number.

G

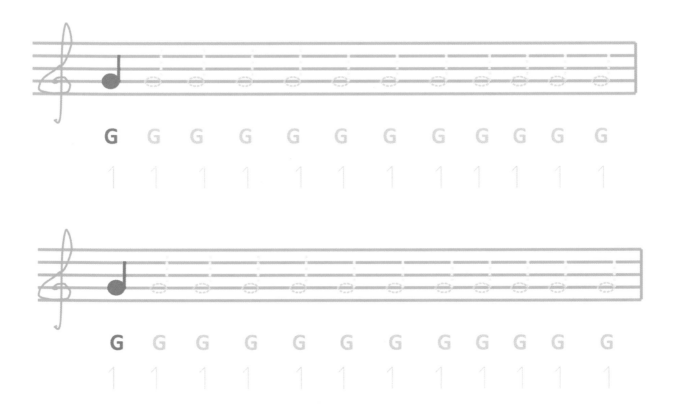

1) Draw a quarter note.
2) Draw a letter.
3) Draw a number.

G

1) Draw a whole, half, quarter note.

C, D, E, F, G

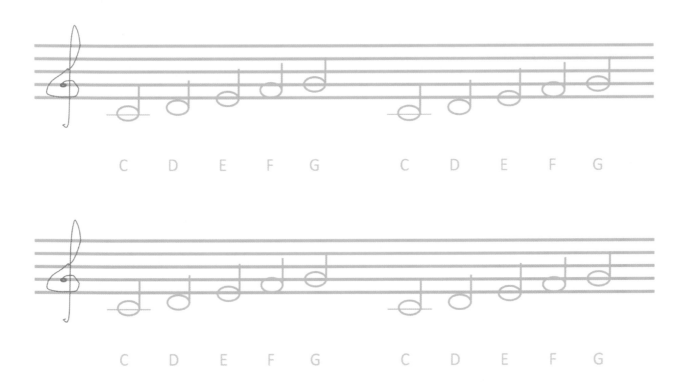

1) Draw quarter notes and the letter names.

C, D, E, F, G

1) Draw quarter notes and the letter names.

C, D, E, F, G

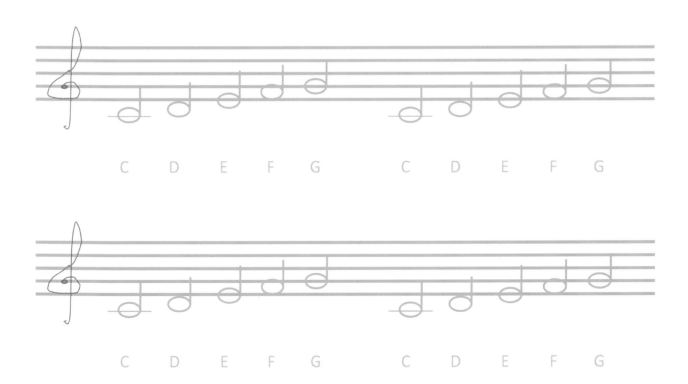

1) Draw quarter notes and the letter names.

C, D, E, F, G

1) Draw quarter notes and the letter names.

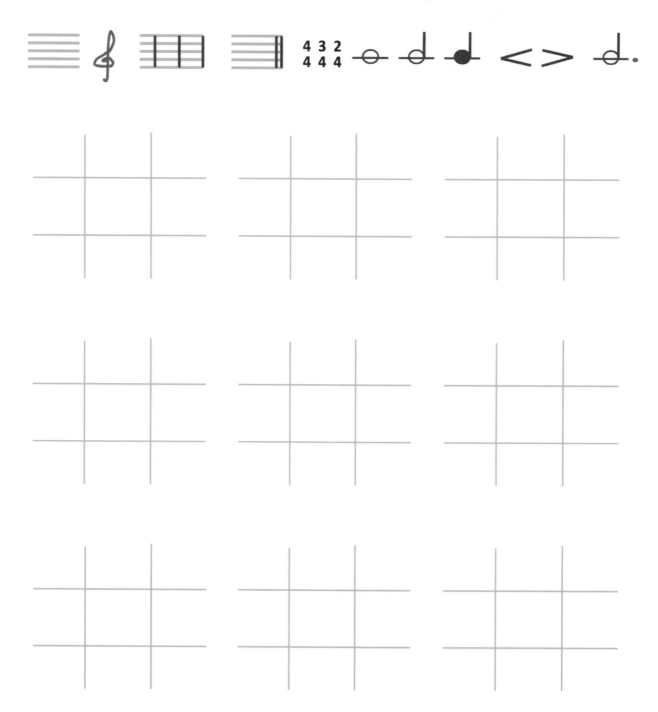

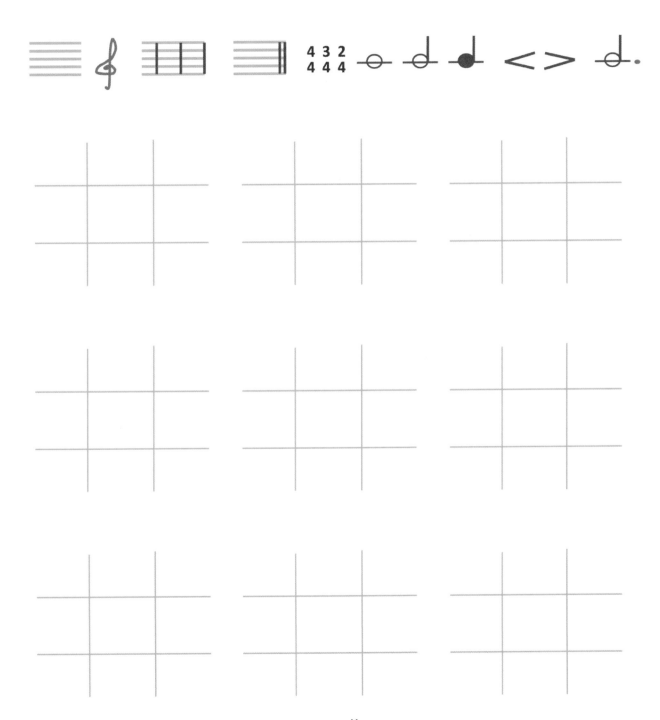

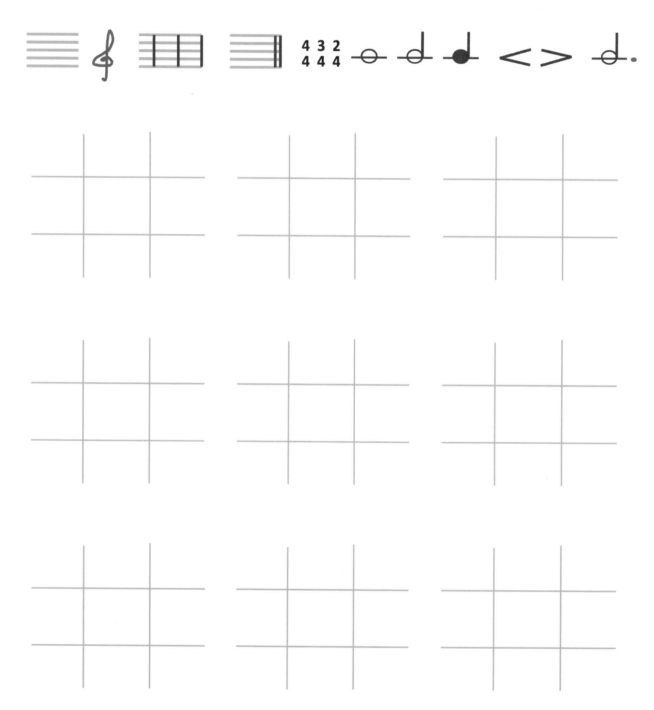

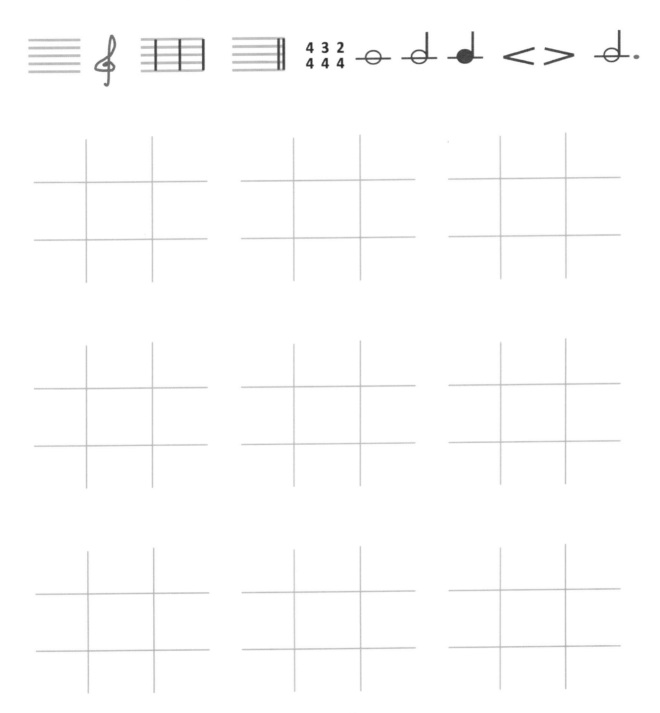

Certificate

This is to certify that

_____

successfully completed

Magic work book A-B

on

_____

and is eligible for promotion to

Magic work book 1A-1B

Congratulations!

_____

Teacher's signature

This course is carefully leveled into the following books :

Magic piano book for 4 year olds - Primer Level A	ISBN-13: 978-1490375946
Magic piano book for 4 year olds - Primer Level B	ISBN-13: 978-1490997391
Magic work book for 4 year olds - Primer Level A-B	ISBN-13: 978-1490997780
Magic piano book - Level 1A - For Beginners	ISBN-13: 978-1499722758
Magic piano book - Level 1B - For Beginners	ISBN-13: 978-1499723243
Magic work book - Level 1A-1B - For Beginners	ISBN-13: 978-1499723816
Magic piano book - Level 2A	ISBN-13: 978-1490999050
Magic piano book - Level 2B	ISBN-13: 978-1490999111
Magic work book - Level 2A-2B	ISBN-13: 978-1490999159
Sinterklaasliedjes – Niveau 2	ISBN-13: 978-1499724202

Made in the USA
Las Vegas, NV
07 June 2021

24289442R00033